Walk by Faith
(Page 3)

To include,

Walk on the Water
(Page 11)

What Are You Doing?
(Page 18)

What is Truth?
(Page 25)

Neville Goddard

Copyright © 2017 Watchmaker Publishing

ISBN 978-1-60386-747-4

Walk *by* Faith

lake asked the question: "Why is it that the Bible is more entertaining and instructive than any other book? Is it not because it is addressed to the Imagination, which is spiritual sensation, and only immediately to the understanding, or reason?"

The one book, called the Bible, is composed of sixty-six books. Take this challenge. Read each book as though the depth of your soul is speaking to your surface mind. As though the ineffable Imagination is speaking to the human Imagination, and not to your immediate understanding or reasoning mind.

Let us examine this thought. In his 2nd letter to the Corinthians Paul says: "We walk by faith and not by sight." When we walk by sight, we know our way by objects that the eye sees. But Paul tells us to order our life by objects seen only in the imagination. In other words, when you know where you want to go and what you want to be, you are told not to rearrange your physical structure, but to walk by faith, viewing only the rearranged structure of your mind. And if you will remain faithful to that state of consciousness, what is seen only in your imagination will objectify itself in your world.

Paul now adds another observation, saying: "This one thing I do. Forgetting what lies behind, I strain forward to what lies ahead." Paul's goal was the high calling of God in Christ Jesus, but you need not have such a goal. Your desire could be a successful business. Now, everything begins in the imagination, for man is all imagination and God is man. God and man differ only in the degree of imagination's intensity. Now keyed low, man walks by sight or by faith in his human imagination. Walking by sight is easier, because buildings rarely move. But when you walk by faith, the objects in your mind's eye must remain as stable as those of the physical eye.

My brother Victor wanted to be a successful business man, and he knew how to remain faithful to what he imagined. In 1924, when our family didn't have a cent, Victor rearranged the name on a building (in his mind's eye) to imply we owned it. This he did for two years, when – without any more money than when he started imagining – a casual acquaintance purchased the building for us without collateral for $50,000. Eight years ago, we sold the building to a bank for $850,000, and there is no capital gains tax in Barbados!

Walking by faith, every day as Victor passed that building, he saw "J. C. Goddard and Sons" on the marquee in place of the existing name of "I. N. Roach & Company". Sight told him the building belonged to another, but faith said the building was his. By simply rearranging the structure of his mind every day for two years, our family's fortune changed.

Now, we are told: "Faith is the assurance of things hoped for; the conviction of things not seen, so that what is seen was made out of things that do not appear."[1] Only my brother Victor saw his mental act. Others saw the sign, "J. N. Roach & Company" – by sight, but Victor saw the words, "J.C. Goddard & Sons" – by faith.

Someone once asked Blake what he saw when he looked at the sun, and he replied, "I see a host of angels singing, 'Holy, Holy, Holy, Lord God Almighty.'" We can all see the same tree but see it differently, just as we can the same man. One may see him in need, while another sees him gainfully employed, both using the same power. You have the power to either live by faith or by sight. If you live by sight, accepting everything that happens, you remain an automaton, unable to change the conditions and events in your world. Only as you begin to live by faith will your life change.

Paul tells us that no matter what he has done or did not do, he puts it behind him and stretches forward towards what lies

---

[1] Hebrews 11 -

ahead. Paul's ideal was to be called to the highest point of God. I hope this is your ideal, too, but perhaps it is not. Maybe other things are pressing upon you, such as the need for money. If so, make that your objective, but use the same technique.

Put the past behind you. Do not look back and become like Lot's wife who turned into a pillar of salt – which is a preservative. You always put what you want to preserve in brine. If you turn back and dwell upon the state you want to leave behind, you have placed it in brine and will become it once more. But if you will turn your back upon the past regardless of what you have or have not done, and stretch forward to what you want to be or do and remain faithful to your desire – nothing can stop you from achieving it. You will become the man you assume you are, if you persist in the assumption that you are already there!

Like Blake, I have found the Bible most entertaining, challenging, and instructive. It is not an easy book to read, however. If it were, it would not be worth my care, for as the ancients discovered, that which is not too explicit is fittest for instruction, as it rouses the faculties to act.

Take this simple statement in Hebrews: "In many and various ways God spoke of old to our fathers by the prophets, but in these last days he has spoken to us by his son who reflects the glory of God and bears the stamp of his nature."

The prophets, instruments through which God spoke, recorded their visions of what God intended, saying: "The heavens declare the glory of God and the firmament shows forth his handiwork."[2] But in the last days God speaks to us by his son, David. This is a fantastic revelation, for in the end God is going to reveal himself.

I could tell you until the ends of time that you are He, but only David can make you believe it. I'll tell you why. Many

---

[2] Psalms 18 & 19

people, like Bishop Pike, question the authority of scripture; but it will never be questioned after it is experienced.

In the Book of Revelation, Jesus Christ is called "the word of God". And in the Book of John he declares his word is truth. May I tell you: only when a truth is experienced can it be known. I know what I have experienced is true. You have heard my words and believe me, but you will not know their truth to the degree that I do until they are experienced.

I have told you how my brother walked by faith rather than by sight, and created a fabulous business in the islands. Sight told him he didn't have a penny to his name. But in faith he began to alter his life by that which only his imagination could see. Your sight registers what is before you right now. If you do not like it, you have an "I" within that is Christ in you. He is the power of imagination which, through faith, can change your life.

As the operant power of your imagination, you can tell where you are going and what you are doing by watching your thoughts. If certain events in your past are unlovely and you remember them, you are ordering their experience. But if you turn your back on the past by forgetting what lies behind and stretch forward to what lies ahead, you will order your conversations aright and become what you behold. This truth will never be disproved, but you are its operant power and must live by it. You need nothing on the outside, but can start just where you are; but you must walk in the direction you set up in your imagination.

Ask yourself this simple question: What would it be like if it were true that I am now the person I want to be? Then reach for its feeling, its spiritual sensation. What is that? I'll show you in a very simple way. Feel a piece of glass, now feel a baseball. Does the baseball feel like glass? Can you feel a tennis ball? Does it feel like a baseball or a piece of glass? Can you feel a piece of cloth, a violet, a piano? Do they all feel alike? Of course not.

That's spiritual sensation — a vivid way of seeing, hearing, smelling, tasting, and feeling reality.

A few years ago, I gave a similar lecture in New York City and a lady in my audience decided to test me. While sitting in her chair she embraced a large bunch of roses. She smelled them, felt their velvety petals, and saw their beauty in her mind's eye. Then, breaking the silence, she left my meeting and returned to her hotel room at the Waldorf Astoria.

The next day the queen mother, Queen Elizabeth, was given a party at the Waldorf Astoria, with two thousand people in attendance. After the reception the maître d', not wanting to discard the flowers there, instructed his men to take three dozen roses up to this lady's room. And when she came home that evening, all she could smell were those lovely roses. She had embraced and lost herself in the feeling of the possession of beautiful roses. She walked by faith and not by sight, and the next day her room was filled with the heavenly aroma of roses.

Now, perhaps because of its memory, you find yourself continuing to look back at what you were (and are) and not ahead into what you want to be. If you will order your conversations aright, right now, their truth will happen in the simplest way.

A seamstress and dress designer I know wanted more money. Using her imagination, she held an envelope in her hand and listened to the paper tear as she opened it. Shaking the contents out, she counted the money to the very penny. This she did for seven nights. On the eighth day, a lady called, offering her a job which paid her, to the penny, what she had imagined. Do you know — that lady could have counted out much more and she would have received it, but she was quite satisfied with the amount she had imagined.

Now, if there is evidence for a thing, does it matter what the world thinks? Could you ever take this lady's experience from her? No! The truth, experienced by her parallels scripture, for all things are possible to one who believes. How did this lady believe what she was imagining? She did it by bringing forth all of her senses to bear upon this event. Using her sense of hearing, she heard the paper tear. Shaking the contents of the envelope, she heard the money fall on the table. She felt the envelope and saw the bills inside. Do you know, money has an odor unlike anything else? So, you can smell money. She determined what she would do if she had the money and she did it.

Another lady went to Sterns Department Store in New York City, saying to herself: "Neville says I can have anything I want if I will imagine and believe in my imaginal act." Having no money, this lady walked over to the hat department, took off her hat and tried on a new one. Walking around the area, she admired herself in front of all the mirrors, but when she returned, her hat was gone. When she described it to the sales lady, she learned that her hat had been sold! The section manager was called in, and he told her to take any hat she wanted, compliments of Sterns. She liked the one she had been wearing, so she left the store with her new hat on her head, and she hadn't paid a dime for it.

Here is another story of a similar nature. This lady's profession was that of being a lady of the evening. She attended all of my meetings, and one day she said to me; "You know, Neville, the strangest thing happened. You told me that I could have anything I wanted if I simply imagined it.

One day I saw a beautiful hat in the window of a department store on Broadway. It was $18, but I loved it so I imagined wearing the hat. As I walked up the street I kept looking at my reflection in the shop windows, seeing that hat on my head. Arriving home, I imagined placing the new hat in the closet instead of my old one. Every day, for the next week or ten days, as I put on my old hat, I imagined it was the new one. Then one day a friend called and asked me to come see her. While there, she brought out a hat box and said; 'I must have been insane when I bought this hat. I wouldn't wear it to a dog fight; yet strangely enough I feel it would look lovely on you.' She opened the box and brought out, not a hat, but the hat, the very hat I had seen in the window and worn in my imagination." Then she asked: "Neville, why didn't God give me the money to buy the hat myself, instead of giving it to me in this manner?"

Knowing her profession, I said, "Ann, do you owe any rent?" and she replied, "Yes, two weeks." "What do you pay, about $17.50 per week?" "Yes." "So, you owe $35. What price hats do you usually buy? Three or four-dollar ones? Have you ever bought a $17 hat?" "Never." "Then tell me honestly. If, when you were looking at the hat, you had seen a $100 bill on the ground, would you have brought the hat?" She said "No." Then I said, "No matter how much money God might have given you, you still would not have bought the hat, so someone else had to buy it for you, and they did."

I have bought clothes, brought them home, and wondered what possessed me to buy them. I did it because someone was treading in the winepress elsewhere. Someone imagined a suit of clothes, so I went to my tailor, chose the cloth, and paid for the suit. But when I brought it home, my wife wouldn't let me bring it into the house. Then a friend who wanted something just like it contacted me and got the suit. He was treading the winepress while I paid for the suit.

Believe me, imagination is spiritual sensation. It is a vivid sight, a vivid sound. When Beethoven went deaf, all sound to the outer ear came to its end. Then Beethoven began to hear with the inner ear and wrote all of the beautiful music we so enjoy.

You can now think of someone you love and hear him speak. If you can't hear him, use one of your other spiritual senses. A touch, a sound, a sight, or an odor will do. I know in New York City, years ago, as I walked through Harlem, I smelled the odor of cooking that instantly took me to Barbados. Although I was physically in Harlem, my sense of smell told me I was 2000 miles away in Barbados.

You can remember a sound, a touch, a sight, and put yourself any place. Like Paul, learn to walk by faith and not by sight. Forget what lies behind and stretch forward to what lies ahead. In the third chapter of Philippians, Paul names his desire as the calling of God in Christ Jesus, but it need not be yours.

I urge you to try this, for your life is forever. Nothing dies. The little rose that blooms once blooms forever, for nothing passes away. If a loved one ceases to be in this little sphere he doesn't die, but is instantly restored to life to carry on his wonderful journey in this age until that moment in time when God speaks to him through his Son, who calls him Father. Only then will he know he is the author of his world. Then his journey will be over, and when he takes off his little garment it will be for the last time.

Paul tells us in Philippians; "I desire to depart and be with Christ, for that is better by far, but it is more necessary that I remain in the flesh on your account." Paul longed to depart and be one with God the Father, but he knew it was necessary for him to remain in the flesh and continue his instruction, just as I do.

Take my words to heart and achieve your every desire. Learn to walk by faith and not by sight and, like Paul, turn your back upon everything you have ever accomplished and go forward – by faith – towards the goal you have set for yourself. Knowing what you would see if your goal were reached, how you would feel if you were there, what you would do now if it were true? Walk in that state and you will achieve it.

Now let us go into the silence.

Walk *on the* Water

he Bible is addressed to the Man of Imagination, he who is immortal and cannot die. "The Eternal Body of Man is the Imagination. That is God Himself. The Divine Body, Jesus, we are his members."[3]

Ted Kennedy recently gave a eulogy for his brother, in which he quoted a passage from George Bernard Shaw. The thought was this: "Some men see things as they are and say, Why? I dream of things that never were and say, Why not?" When you think of your birth into this world as an act of God, can anything be impossible to God? Not knowing how or why you are here, you sin against the Holy Ghost when you dare to put a limit on the power that brought you here! There is no sin against the Holy Ghost other than man's belief that something is impossible to his own wonderful human imagination! I want you to go all out! To put no limit on God's creative power. To imagine that which is unimaginable and to walk on the water, through faith.

Water symbolizes your acceptance of life as psychological, and its drama as taking place in the Imagination. When you cease excusing yourself or anyone for life's experiences, and begin to rearrange the structure of your mind to feel your desire is fulfilled, you are walking on the water. Scripture speaks of the stone, the water, and the wind. Accept the facts of life and you are stepping down on stone. Change the facts in your imagination, and you have turned them into psychological truth, which then becomes a spiritual experience. When you live by this principle, you are walking on water, towards your birth from beyond.

---

[3] William Blake -

Let me now share some experiences of a friend who practices the art of walking on the water. In his letter he said: "There is a lady in my office who was constantly talking about the absence of decent, eligible men in her life, claiming they were all riffraff and no good. Six weeks ago, while driving home from work, I revised her words. I heard her tell me she was dating a marvelous man and sharing the wonderful things they were doing. Recently this lady was so glum, I reminded myself to revise her words again, so I did. Yesterday she spent twenty minutes telling me of the perfect gentleman she is now dating. He must be terrific, for this lady is now walking in ecstasy."

Then he continued, saying: "An associate asked me to write a news review for his client. I gathered all of the material together that I would need, put it in a folder and placed it on my desk, which was piled high with pending work. Then one Friday my associate said: 'My client wants to see me next Monday at 9:00 A.M. in his office,' and I realized that I must produce the news review at that time. Immediately I sat down and imagined it was 5:00 P.M. My review was completed, read by my associate, and approved. I heard him say: 'It is just fine.' Satisfied with that scene as my end result, I found the folder, sat down at my typewriter and typed four pages, as everything flowed smoothly. At 5:00 that afternoon my associate stopped by my office, read the report, and said the exact words I had heard him say in my imagination: 'It is just fine.'"

When you truly believe that imagining creates reality, you will know there is no fiction. How can there be fiction when imagining is forever creating its reality? You may hear something you do not like, but because imagining creates reality what you heard was first imagined, or it could not have happened. When you revise the hearing by stopping the action and rewriting the script you are walking on the water, imagining the reality you desire to hear and appear in your world.

My friend continued his letter, saying: "There are certain things in my life I do not understand. Last Sunday, as my wife, our youngest son, and I were planting summer flowers, I realized that I was experiencing – in detail – what I had dreamed as happening last winter. At the time I thought the dream must have been symbolic, but not knowing the symbolism of flowers, I dropped it. Now I do not understand the relationship between a night dream – which I did not control, and last Sunday's planting – which I did control."

Every event in life contains within itself something beyond its physical experience. Flowers symbolize the growth of plantings. During winter, when nothing grows, he planted seeds, which he will harvest not only in the world of Caesar, but also in the world of the Spirit, as we all do. I urge you now to use your imagination and walk on the water. Plant the seeds of desire in the depth of your soul and allow them to flower on earth. If you do not see their harvest immediately, believe what you did, for it will come whether you recognize it or not. And do not sin against the Holy Ghost by saying something is impossible, for God is your own wonderful human imagination and nothing is impossible to imagine.

When someone tells you something, although you may deny its truth or possibility, you must imagine in order to understand their words. Unless, of course, they speak in a foreign tongue, then all is nonsense. As Paul said: "I would rather speak five words with understanding, than ten thousand words that cannot be understood."

Don't think of the reasons why you cannot have your desire; simply think you already have it! If you tell yourself it is not possible, you are sinning against the Holy Ghost.

I know of no limitation to the power of God. David is described in the Book of Samuel as ruddy, with beautiful eyes, and fair of skin. If you judge from appearance, then certain races would be excluded – but David is not of this world. David is he who rises in us because of the descent of the seed of God. Whether you are Caucasian, Negro, or Oriental, Christ – God's seed – descends and plants itself in you. And when union between that descending, higher seed and that which is only an animated being takes place, you are individually lifted into a supernatural world, where you know yourself to be the father of God's only begotten son, David.

I urge you to use your imagination for everything that is lovely and loving. I don't care what your desire may be – your imagination will give it to you, for the human imagination is the divine body the world calls Jesus. Because you can imagine and I can imagine, we are members of that one divine body, and all things are possible to him. There is not a thing impossible to God. All you need do is imagine its fulfillment!

Faith is an experiment which ends as an experience. Experiment by believing you already have all that you desire, and you will have the experience. Test yourself like my friend did. He experimented with the thought that the lady had a wonderful boyfriend. He then imagined hearing her tell him about the new man in her life. Then his experiment became her experience. You are the center of the world in which you live. A seeming other is only an extension of yourself, for the center of your being is protean. It is he who plays the parts of all the seeming others. I challenge you to experiment with a new or better job, a husband or a wife, a new car or home. Don't try to analyze your desires or blame yourself, for the moment you do, you discover unnumbered things which are unlovely, and the moment they are thought, they are formed.

No one is without sin. At some time, everyone has mentally coveted or stolen. Describe a man in unflattering terms and you have stolen his good name. Everyone is guilty; therefore, do not analyze yourself, for if you do, you will miss your mark. To worry about what you may have done, is to waste your creative power. You will reap the tares as well as the wheat, as every imaginal act fulfills itself. But start now to plant something lovely – not only for yourself, but for your neighbor, friend, or child. Fall in love with the idea that he is happy and secure. Feel the satisfaction that comes when one recognizes his harvest, for if a harvest is not recognized, there is no satisfaction. But when you do something consciously and see your harvest, you will receive enormous satisfaction.

Prove your thoughts have creative power by consciously imaging constantly, and walk on the water. No matter what happens in the course of a day, revise it. Make the day conform to what you want it to be, and you are walking on the water.

Genesis tells the story of Jacob, who saw a well covered with a stone. Removing the stone, he drew water for his flock. And when he put the stone back, everything appeared to remain the same as before, so no one knew who had rolled away the stone and removed the water. In the New Testament, Jesus performed his first miracle by filling the stone jars with water and drawing out wine.

Facts blind the I of imagination. I have come to cure this blindness and show you how to remove the acts of nature. The woman in the office shared her facts, as well as the man who had been bawled out. Discovering imagination to be his well, my friend removed those stone facts from his mind, and drew the truth he desired to hear out of his imagination and placed it in another vessel – another fact. Pour water into any container and it will not care what shape or size the vessel may be. Freeze the container and the water will have taken on its shape. So, if you remove the stone and draw out the water, you can place it into any shape you desire and it will externalize itself.

Do not let a day pass without practicing the art of walking on water. Every time you use your imagination lovingly on behalf of another, you are mediating God to the seeming other. So many people use their imagination un-lovingly, yet they are still mediating God to that other.

Millions of people believe that someone has placed a curse on the Kennedy's. Do you know that such powers do exist, because imagining creates reality. William Butler Yeats once said: "I will never be certain it was not some woman treading in the winepress who started the subtle change in men's mind. Or that the pressing out of which so many countries were given to the sword, did not begin in the mind of some shepherd boy, lighting up his eyes for a moment before it ran upon its way." Who knows who, this night – feeling hurt and betrayed by a friend – will set his thoughts of anger and revenge into motion, with no thought of regret. Perhaps he does not know the art of forgiveness or have the desire to forgive, thereby allowing his thoughts to move and build and build until they come to their inevitable end – by outpicturing themselves in his life. But as George Bernard Shaw said: "Some men see things as they are and say, Why? I see things that never were and say, Why not?" I tell you the incredible story of Jesus Christ, the pattern which man must follow in order to escape eternal death, and say, Why not?

How can we who were physically born by the grace of God, yet cannot make one hair on our head or fingernail grow, dare to put a limit on God's power? If the grace of God gave us physical birth, cannot that same power give us spiritual birth into a higher world? The promise is: "You shall be born from above." If God makes such a promise, he has the power to keep it. And he does, through his gift of vision. Born of flesh by a power beyond ourselves, we are destined to be born into a spiritual world by a power beyond ourselves, because God's seed descended and united with us. It was planted by a creative act; and when that seed is fertilized, it erupts, the pattern awakens, and we move into an entirely different age. God's pattern has erupted in me. I am telling you my story in the hope that you who hear it will believe and prove its truth for yourselves. I have told you of Caesar's law, taught you how to walk on the water and use this psychological law to change your world – not only for yourselves, but for others.

No one needs to remain behind the proverbial eight-ball if he knows this truth. There is no need to beg or ask anyone for anything, for everything lives in the human imagination, ready to appropriate and be made visible.

Everyone will be born from above, for everyone is God and there is nothing but God. No one can fail; but God's story must be heard and believed. So, God sends himself as the messenger, by choosing an individual and impregnating him. The person may or may not know what is happening, but in the perfect interval of time, birth will take place. Everyone here is called for a purpose. If you have not been united with this seed – wait, for it is sure and will not be late. There are those who have been conscious when they received the seed. Others have not; but when the child is born does it matter whether the moment of conception is remembered or not?

It's all the fulfillment of a perfect plan within God's eternal body, each filling his specific order. There are those who will be the apostle, others the prophet, still others the teacher, the helper, and the healer. There are different levels in the body of God, but it doesn't matter, because in that body we are all one.

Take me seriously. When you know what you want in life, construct a scene which would imply your desire is fulfilled. See it as clearly as possible. Feel its naturalness. Experiment until you know the scene and all it implies is real. Now, to the degree that you believe in its reality, your experiment will become your experience. Do not stop there. Keep on imagining and share your results with others. Tell them how to free themselves from this bondage to Caesar.

When you know who you really are, you will not envy anyone. How could you, when you know you are God, and they are only yourself pushed out? If tomorrow, something comes into your life that is not to your liking, do not accept it, for this fact blinds the I of imagination. Remove the blindness by asking yourself what you would like, in place of what seems to be. Enter into that thought. Revel in it as though it were not a fact. Persuade yourself that it is. Believe in its reality and it will become your experience.

Now let us go into the silence.

What Are You Doing?

any times I have heard someone say: "I believe that imagining creates reality, but I once imagined something and it never came to pass." Then I ask: "What are you doing, saying: 'I once imagined it' and not imagining it now? For God's name is I Am, not I did! Always thinking of God as someone outside of himself, man finds it difficult to keep the tense, but God is the human imagination and there is no other God.

When you imagine you may include others, but do not think in terms of influence. Rather, think only in terms of clarity of form.

Perhaps a friend would like a better job, more money, and greater responsibility. Before you imagine, take a moment and clarify the form your imaginal act will take. Are you giving the celebration party, or is he? Who will be there? Fill the room with those who would want to share in the celebration. Raise your glass and say: "Here's to your fabulous new job, your salary increase, and the challenge of your greater responsibility!" Don't think in terms of trying to influence the friend's boss, for he could die or be discharged. Just go to the end. Toast the event, and do not think of influencing others.

The law, to be effective, needs feeling with form. Build a structure that would imply your desire is already fulfilled, and enter its form with feeling. You do not have to be concerned about influencing others, as they are not the cause – your imaginal act is! Those who have a billion dollars are not causing your world. You and you alone are doing it, as your imaginal acts influence people. Everyone is yourself pushed out, so when you imagine, you are influencing yourself!

Knowing what you want, place your attention on its clarity of form, and then watch what you are imagining. Are you remembering when you imagined something greater than what you have? If so, you are confessing you are not now imagining your desire fulfilled. If imagining creates reality, you must change your memory and become aware of what you are imagining right now.

Let me now tell you of a series of dreams I received from a friend. The series began one night when she found herself with a group of children, trying to find something that was lost. Seeing a brown paper bag tied with string, she opened it and removed a watch, as one of the children said: "That is a treasure," and the dream ended.

The next night she found herself moving as if on wheels, with everything she sees moving with her. Then she said to herself: "This is not what I want. Everything is moving, while I still have the sense of longing," and she awoke.

The following night, she felt herself walking with an enormous crowd across fields, on roads, and sidewalks. She went up hills and down stairs, attending my lectures in many places. Listening attentively, she was thrilled to hear the revelations which were being shared. Entering a beautiful, old, ivy-covered building, she tried to mentally remember every word I said; but when she awoke on her bed, their memory was gone.

The next night she entered an expansive white house, which she knew her father had built. All of the rooms were empty, except the one in which I was teaching and the adjacent room where her father was. (Don't forget this aspect of the dream, as the father is unseen.) Addressing all of my remarks to her, she is filled with joy. Then, with profound authority I announced: "My name is Friday." Recognizing its tremendous significance, she said: "Yes! And that means, O my darling." I smiled, nodded, and she awoke.

My friend heard and saw correctly, for my name is Friday, as I am the God of love. In mythology (which is only part vision) love is a goddess. But in vision, love is man. Having been incorporated into the body of the Risen Lord, I am the embodiment of love; I am one with that one body, one Spirit, one Lord, one God and Father of all.

The word "*yachid*" is used only ten or twelve times in scripture. It is defined as "my darling, my only son". Anyone who is incorporated into the body of love is *yachid*, and called my darling. The word first appears in the 22nd chapter of Genesis, when the Lord – speaking of the promised child – says to Abraham: "You did not withhold your only son (*yachid*)," Then, in the Gospel of John, when the crucifixion and resurrection had taken place, this passage from Zechariah is quoted: "They shall look upon him whom they have pierced, and mourn for him as one mourns for an only child (*yachid*)."[4] I have experienced scripture. I now tell its truth to those who will listen. Those who believe my words will encounter me as I teach night after night. My friend could not recall the words I spoke, but she did remember my name, for my name is Friday, as I am the God of love.

The first definition given to the word *yachid* is unity; sole (in the sense of being unique); the only one. Everyone incorporated into that one body is unique and the only one, for there is only one body, only one Spirit, only one Lord, only one God and Father of us all. In that body there is a unity, yet an individuality; and when you wear it you are Friday, the God of love.

On this level no one sees that body, but she saw it in the spirit and brought the memory of the experience back with her. In the ivy-covered walls I instructed others, but in the white house there was only one door to the room occupied by her unseen father and where I spoke to her alone. Do you see the symbolism?

---

[4] John 19 & Zechariah 12 -

Now a dream is egocentric, with every aspect of it taking place in the individual. Although the dream unfolds in one, that one contains all. In her dream the father is unseen, but projects himself into the teacher – who tells her that her father is the God of love.

Returning to this level, the first words given us by the one who comes to reveal this truth – that imagining creates reality – are: "Repent and believe in the gospel." Repentance, which is a radical change of attitude, can cause your powerful imagination to burst through this world of death. So, I ask you to repent. To test this wonderful law by changing your attitude towards life and watch what happens.

A gentleman recently dreamed he was peeling his head, bringing the skin down to his neck then pulling it back again. As he did, he realized that he was generating light from the inside and knew that the outside was completely dark. This gentleman saw the truth. Blake said it so beautifully: "All that you behold, though it appears without it is within, in your imagination of which this world of mortality is but a shadow." Now he knows that the outer world is being lit by the light of awareness which comes from within.

While listening to a taped lecture of mine, this gentleman fell asleep and was awakened by two terrific blows on the right side of his head and saw the index finger of the right hand extended. Having peeled his head, he has removed the outer skin of Esau. Knowing he must continue to wear it while here, this gentleman will put it back on; but now he knows the world is made alive from within – and that in itself is quite a blow. This man has been coming to hear me for only a short time. He has appeared at the eleventh hour and is receiving the same fruit as those who came at the first hour. Everyone receives the same message and the same blows, as they are essential to the awakening of the sleeping one within all.

In his wonderful hymn, Isaac Watts says: "Wrapped within the silence of the tomb the great redeemer sleeps. Hail and death combined their force to hold our Lord, but the great conqueror arose and broke the fragile chain." Your heavenly Father sleeps within you as your own wonderful human Imagination. One day He will break the chain and you will rise as He! But in the meantime, put him to the test, and you will discover that neither hail nor death combining their force will keep your desires from being fulfilled.

Now, there is an eternal brotherhood and fatherhood, for every individual is the father of the same child. How would I ever know that you and I are one were it not for this symbol? God placed eternity (his only son, David) in the mind that man may know he is his father. And if you know David to be your son, and I know I am his father, are we not one? There is no other way of proving our brotherhood, save through our common fatherhood.

If you had a son and I had another, we could question this common fatherhood; but there is only one son, who is loved by all. We are all one, but we will know it only as we are gathered into that one body, one Spirit, one Lord, one God and Father of all.

Always think in clarity of form, for as you do, you are influencing others. When I wanted to get out of Barbados, I didn't think of influencing anyone. I simply used clarity of form and walked up the gangplank in my imagination. That act caused someone five thousand miles away to cancel their passage. And although there were hundreds ahead of me waiting for passage, the one who had the power to distribute the tickets chose us, so I did influence others. I imagined, and we came back, while thousands who preceded us in applying for passage continued to wait their turn.

Do you know that the moment you draw a line you encompass energy? That without an outline, everything is nothing? Draw your outline and make your picture as clear as possible. Perhaps you are giving a party to honor one who is present. Sit at the table with friends and raise your glass.

Congratulate your friend on his new position, his greater salary and more responsibility. Stick to that thought, and it will not matter to you who is influenced.

The moment you think of influence, you reduce a miracle to magic. All the people in the world are only yourself pushed out. No one has the power to hold you back or promote you, for you are self-promoted or self-restricted.

Blake tells us to enter into – not just observe, but enter into – images in our imagination. To approach them on the fiery chariot of contemplative thought. To make a friend and companion of any one of these images of wonder, for if we will, we will rise from the grave and meet the Lord in the air and be happy.

Let us say you are in Los Angeles and want to be in New York City. You could enter the city on the fiery chariot of your contemplative thought by thinking from it, and no longer thinking from Los Angeles. You enter New York City by rising from your grave of flesh and blood in Los Angeles and meeting your Lord (your I AM) in the air. Do that and you will be happy in the doing, for that is how reality is created.

When you enter the state, you desire to express and believe it is true, no earthly power can stop it from objectifying itself. And although you do not deliberately influence others, you influence everyone. As Sir James Frazer said: "A man on this planet cannot raise a hand without influencing the farthest star in the heavens in its unified form."

Practice the art of imagining, and you will discover you can go anywhere and enter any time without the aid of anyone. Move in your imagination, and people will respond because of your action. Dare to assume you are wealthy, and watch everyone play their parts to provide you with the wealth you claim to have. They will, for they are only yourself pushed out.

The world goes on and on, as the actors – playing their numberless parts – desire more and more things that vanish. Man is forever fighting for something that passes away; yet he is told: "Do not lay up treasures on earth where thieves can take and the moth corrupt, but lay up treasures in heaven where no man can take from you."

The treasures of earth can be withdrawn at any moment, but the treasures in the instructions I am giving you now are forever. Only one being was pierced, and that is Jesus Christ, your true identity. The crucifixion is over. You have been crucified with Christ, and your resurrection will take place in you, in its own wonderful time.

I ask you to test your imagination! Go all out and believe in what you have imagined. Do not try to influence anyone. Instead, put all of your energies into clarity of form.

If a certain desk designates that you are occupying a desired position, occupy that desk. Enter into the image, and you will realize your vision. Sit in the chair behind that desk and view the room. Persist in thinking from that point of view. If you do not physically occupy that chair tomorrow, and begin to doubt, ask yourself: "What am I doing, remembering and not imagining?" Then return to your chair behind that desk!

Now let us go into the silence.

What *is* Truth?

hristianity is the fulfillment of Judaism, the fulfillment of all that was prophesied in the Old Testament. This week the Christian world celebrates Passover, the triumphal march into Jerusalem – the trial, the crucifixion, burial, and resurrection. Let me share these events with you as they are seen through the eyes of one who has experienced them.

In the 18th chapter of the Book of John, Pilate said: "So you are a king?" and Jesus replied: "You say that I am, but my kingdom is not of this world. For this I was born. For this I came into the world, to bear witness to the truth." Then Pilate asked: "What is truth?" and when there was no response, Pilate left, saying: "I find nothing in this man worth condemnation." Having already claimed: I am the truth, and my word is truth, here we find Jesus making the claim: I came to bear witness to the truth.

Peter tells us that "The prophets who prophesied of the grace that was to be yours searched and inquired concerning this salvation. They inquired what person or time was indicated by the spirit of Christ in them, when predicting the suffering of Christ and the subsequent glory. It was revealed to them that they were serving not themselves, but you."

The prophets were doing a work, the full import of which was in the promise. They were conditioned to hear – and quite often to see – the word of God. Although they recorded what they heard, they did not understand the writing. Daniel declared: "I heard but did not understand." Then he was told to "Shut up the words and seal the book until the time of the end." The time when the word, embodied in flesh, unfolds in a man who – having broken the seal – interprets the written word from experience. He came into the world and the world knew him not. Even today the word is still misunderstood.

Hundreds of millions of Christians will go to church this coming Friday and the following Sunday, to proclaim Christ has risen; yet they do not know the Word. But when he who is sent by love enters the world, he finds a small group who will accept his words. From that group, an even smaller group will understand him to the point of complete acceptance.

Scripture is completely misunderstood and can be interpreted only by one who is called, incorporated into the body of love, and sent back into this world of death to await that moment in time when the word unfolds from within. And when he tells his experiences, the multitude cannot believe him, for it is not what they were taught; yet, having become an eyewitness, he can no longer say "I think", or "I believe," as our theologians do. His is an assured "I know!" To believe in something is marvelous, but it cannot be known until it is experienced.

Many years ago, I was a dancer in New York City. One day I took a taxi from rehearsal to my hotel. When we arrived, the driver claimed I had broken the glass when I slammed the door, and asked me to pay for it. I knew I had not broken any glass and suspected he had been collecting $8 from every fare all through the day, so I did not pay him other than what the meter read, plus a generous tip. A short time after I had retired to my room, the phone rang, and the operator said that there was a policeman in the lobby who wanted to see me. When we met, he asked me about the broken glass, and I told him I had not done it. It was the dinner hour, so I was asked to go with him to the night court. This I did, and when the driver was asked if he knew I had broken the glass and he said: I think he did – the case was dismissed. He thought I did it and maybe he believed it, but he did not know! One must have an assured I know, which can only be obtained from experience.

I stand before you knowing the truth, and it is not as it will be re-enacted this coming week in all of the Christian churches of the world. Christ in you is your hope of glory. One day – like a tree – that living word will bloom in you and bear its visionary fruit, all related to the Old Testament.

The only Bible that the early Christians had was the Old Testament. Those who wrote the New Testament were called "the people of the way". Do you know who they were? Jews! Although the unknown authors of the books Matthew, Mark, Luke, and John were Jews, they did not confess that they were, like Paul did. Paul's 13 letters, which form the bulk of the New Testament, came first. It was he who said; "I am a Jew, a child of Abraham of the tribe of Jacob." Paul never denied his Jewish ancestry, yet he laid the foundation of the Christian faith. Man forgets this, and thinks the Old and New Testaments represent two religions; but there is only one religion, whose foundation is Judaism and fulfillment (like the fruit appearing on a tree) is Christianity.

This is the greatest story that has ever been told. The crucifixion is over. I know, for I remember when I – a whirling vortex – crucified myself upon this body called Neville at six points: the hands, the feet, the head, and the right side. The Word of God, who is God, is nailed to your body by whirling vortices. This is the same Word who was in the beginning with God and was God. There was meaning in that Word, a plan, and a purpose, which was revealed to you before the world began. This is not some emergency thinking on the part of God; he chose us in him before that the world was!

Christ is in us, crucified on our body. He became a slave that your body may be alive, and he will wear that body until he awakens. The body you now wear can be cremated and therefore gone from the mortal eye; yet you, its wearer, are still very much alive, continuing your act of slavery in a body just like the one you now wear. In my own case, however, I will not wear a body of death any longer; for the Word has erupted within me. I know scripture is true from beginning to end, for I have experienced it. I also know that those in whom it has not erupted will find themselves restored to life.

If our late president Eisenhower has not had the Word unfold within him, even though he was the president of our great country, he has been restored to life as a young man, about 20 years of age. He will be in a terrestrial world like this one, in an environment best suited to his needs, to continue the work that was started in him by the son of God, who is his ancestral self.

When I speak of the son of God, I am referring to man's true being. No child enters this world unless a son of God – who is his ancestral self – supports him by dreaming him into being. And everyone who leaves this section of time moves into another section of time automatically, until his ancestral self-awakens.

The only purpose of life is to bear witness to the truth of the Old Testament, which is the word of God. God's word has erupted in me. Having fulfilled the prophecy of the Old Testament, I bear witness to its truth. The Old Testament is the prophecy, but dead until it erupts. Then the individual within whom it erupts becomes Jesus, the Spirit of prophecy. Men have speculated on the meaning of the Old Testament, and will believe their speculations from now until the ends of time; but they will not know the truth until it erupts within them. You may trust one in whom it has happened. You may believe he is telling the truth and adjust your thinking to conform to his words; but you cannot know their truth until you individually experience it. To believe the words of another are true is not good enough. The judge will throw out the case unless the witness can say, I know! For it happened in me!

This week the trial, the crucifixion, burial, and death of God's creative power will be celebrated – but not the other side of the coin of resurrection, which is the birth. Christianity is an Easter religion. Without resurrection, Christianity would just be another little ism. The world is full of little isms and they are all helpful. Being psychological, they encourage positive thinking, telling you how to assume a certain attitude of mind and live a freer, healthier, more wonderful life. But when it comes to truth, Christianity is the religion of Easter, the religion of rising from the world of death and entering the world of life, called the kingdom of heaven. It is the story of the salvation of the gods who came down.

In the Book of Deuteronomy, we are told that bounds have been set to the peoples of the earth according to the number of the sons of God. A child could not know life here, were it not for his ancestral self, who is one of the Sons of God who fell as one Man. Containing all men within the one, all will return to that one Man – but each in his own good time. No one can tell when that hour will come. You may long for it, but you cannot force its coming.

While on the cross, Jesus said: "I thirst." You may think he is thirsting for water, but his thirst was caused by the famine which is sent upon the land. It is not a hunger for bread or a thirst for water, but for the hearing of the word of God. Thirsting, they gave him vinegar, in the fulfillment of the 69th Psalm, "...for my thirst they gave me vinegar to drink." Having come into the world only to bear witness to the truth, I know God's word is truth! When his word becomes alive in you, the Old Testament will erupt like a seed, and you will know the truth of scripture from experience. Then you will tell the world, who will receive you not, because they will know your physical background and not the Word of God who unfolded within you. Only one who has fulfilled the Word can interpret scripture. The prophets wrote it, but they could not understand their writing. The scribes – not understanding – lived by the external word; but experience brings the internal Word to match the external one.

It is said that two different persons must agree in testimony for the testimony to be conclusive. The two can be the external

What is Truth?

word of scripture, and the internal Word unfolding within the individual. If they agree, their testimony is conclusive.

When he said: "For this I was born," he was not speaking of a physical birth, but of a spiritual one; for unless you are born from above, you cannot enter the kingdom of God. Man, born into the world of Caesar, lives with reason and logic. To him one must be born as an offspring from the womb of a woman; yet Jesus is speaking of an entirely different birth – the birth of Spirit, which comes from above, and not the birth of flesh, which comes from below.

His statement continues, "For this I came into the world." This is true, for the Word became flesh, as you and I, and now dwells within us. "He is clothed in a robe drenched in blood, and his name is called the Word of God." Is not the body you now wear drenched in blood? Our Cardinals wear red robes and call themselves princes of the church, but that is not the robe spoken of here. Every child born of woman wears the red robe as his body of flesh and blood. Incarnating himself, the Word is made flesh and dwells in us all.

You are the incarnated Word of God, who at one moment in time will be called. Your name, already written in the Book of Life, will be checked off; and you will be incorporated into the living body of love, which is God's most radiant form. In that instant you become one with that same body, that same Spirit, that same Lord, that one God and Father of all.

As Love, yet wearing a body of power, you will be sent back into the world to wait your time of thirty years. While here, you will do all of the normal things you did before. You will make mistakes, you will laugh and cry, and then suddenly scripture will erupt from within, and you will find yourself compelled to tell your experiences to all who will listen. But because it is not what tradition teaches, many will turn their back and walk away, unable to believe what they cannot comprehend.

This Friday, many will spend three hours celebrating an event which took place in me in the matter of moments; for I remember the night memory returned, and I reenacted the 42nd Psalm. I remember when I walked in procession to the house of God, when a voice rang out saying: "And God walks with them." A woman questioned the voice, saying: "If God walks with us, where is he?" and the voice replied: "At yours side." Turning to her right, she looked into my eyes and laughed, because she saw a man she knew was weak and frail, a man who could succumb to temptation. Her question: "What? Neville is God?" was answered: "Yes, in the act of waking." Then the voice spoke to me from the depth of my soul, and said: "I laid myself down within you to sleep, and as I slept I dreamed a dream... Suddenly I knew exactly what he was dreaming, for in a split second I felt myself become vortices, as I penetrated my hands, my feet, my head, and the right side of my body. I felt the six points of the Mogen David, the Star of David, experiencing an ecstasy greater than my wildest dreams. Now I know the crucifixion happened on the night of the triumphal journey into Jerusalem. Tradition is correct in keeping it in the same time slot, but they do not tell the story correctly.

In the Book of Acts, we find this quote from Deuteronomy: "Cursed be anyone who hangs upon a tree." The crucifixion took place upon the tree of life, in Man, and not on any wooden tree. Blake tells us so beautifully:

> *"The gods of the earth and sea*
> *Sought through nature to find this tree.*
> *But their search was all in vain;*
> *There grows one in the human brain."*

Look at a picture of the human body with the skin removed, and you will see all of the veins and arteries rooted in the brain and turned down into generation. That is the tree spoken of in the Book of Daniel. It was felled, stripped of its leaves, and its fruit was scattered. The root, however, was not to be interfered with. After seven times pass over, and the one who was felled knows that the Most High rules the kingdom of men and gives it to whom he will, the tree is reversed; and its energy will move from generation to regeneration, as it bursts into bloom and bears its glorious fruit.

In that crucified state we fell and crucified ourselves on the living tree, which was felled. Its root is the human imagination, which will awaken in the holy sepulcher, where the drama began. You see, it is there that God entered death's door and lay down in the grave of man to dream the dream of life. It is there that He will awaken. It is there that He will come out and look back upon that which contained him that body of a slave.

Then all of the imagery of his birth from above will appear, so that He can make the statement: "For this I was born; for this I came into the world: to bear witness to the truth. Thy Word is truth." The written word is a sealed book of which I, the living Word, interpret through experience.

True scriptural interpretation can never be gained through learning. Knowledge must be obtained from experience. Learning may cause you to think it is true; but you can only know scriptural truth through experience. When the story of Christianity has fulfilled itself in you, you do not have to believe in the Christian faith – you know it is true! And Christianity is the fulfillment of Judaism. It is man's departure from this world of death and his entrance into the world of life! After the Word has erupted in you, you will wear a garment of death no more.

No one ever really dies, because the immortal Word is in him. A friend may appear to die, but he does not. He is instantly restored as a living being without change of identity, where he will continue his journey until God's word becomes activated and lives in him. And when it does, he becomes a witness to the written word of scripture.

The Word doesn't come to change Caesar's world. It is the Risen Word who says: Render unto Caesar the things that are Caesar's and unto God the things that are God's. If Caesar wants taxes, give them to him. If you desire things in Caesar's world, assume you have them and Caesar will be satisfied, for you will have them. You can always meet Caesar's demands. If he wants something else; don't quarrel with him, simply assume he has it. You don't change Caesar, for he is just as much a slave as you are. Whether he be a king or a Pope, man is still a slave to the body he wears, and cannot compel anyone to digest, assimilate, or eliminate, for him. He has to do it all by himself. And when he dies to this world, he is restored to find himself in a body that is just as much a slave as this one.

Those who have gone beyond are now performing the normal, natural functions of the body. There is sex there, hate, and love – just as here. It's the same world, for your life does not terminate at the point where your senses cease to register it. Like a play on Broadway, you may leave the stage, but you remain the actor. Having left the stage, you are no longer seen by the actors who remain there; but your identity does not change. It goes on forever.

The drama is concentrated this week; but the truth is not being told, as man finds it easier to see thought in picture form. But in the story of salvation – Jesus Christ – is publicly portrayed as crucified. The portrayal began in the spirit! It never existed in the flesh. Haven't you gone to the theater and become so carried away with the acting that you forgot the message the actor was trying to portray? Many a play is not just for amusement, but to educate. Such is the story of salvation. It is the greatest play that was ever conceived, but man has fallen in love with the husk, because he does not know the kernel. That is why Paul made the statement:" Who has bewitched you, before whose eyes Jesus Christ was publicly portrayed as crucified? Let me ask you only this: Did you receive the spirit by works of the law or by hearing with faith? Are you so foolish that you have turned from the spirit to the flesh? From now on regard no one after the flesh, even though I once regarded Christ from the human point of view, I regard him thus no longer.

This week Christians will celebrate a physical death, and Christ is not and never was a physical being. They will celebrate the ascension of an individual, yet Christ is universal. The Cosmic Christ is buried in every child born of woman. And that Cosmic Christ is represented by the sons of God, who altogether form the Lord God Jehovah. Every child possesses an ancestral self, who is an individualized son of God, who will awaken to reveal the true identity of that child. Right now, your ancestral self is individualized as you. And one day you, too, will know who you are. No one on earth knows your true identify; but you will know it, for you will return to your ancestral self that was – and still is – one of the sons of God. The word *Elohim* is a compound unity of one made up of others. We are the *Elohim* (pron. e-lo-HEEM) which form YAD HE VAU HE (pron. "YOD HEY VAV HEY"), the lord. Not one of us can be absent, for it takes all of us to make the whole.

Remember: Jesus Christ is not a little man, but the Cosmic Christ who dwells in you and will erupt in you, causing you to return to the one body, the one Spirit, the one Lord, the one God and Father of all. I am telling you what I know is truth. Our theologians recite creeds. They share their knowledge as to what they have learned and thereby believe; but they cannot tell you what they know until they have the experience. I tell you that you are God the Father; but you will never know it until you meet your one and only begotten son, whose name is David. You cannot come into the knowledge that you are God the Father except by him. "No one knows who the Father is except the son, and no one knows who the son is except the Father." When the living word begins to unfold, the Son you have been searching for throughout eternity will appear. Then you will know the truth and these words will become yours, "For this I was born. For this I came into the world: to bear witness to the truth!"

When the personification of reason asked: What is truth? the personification of truth did not answer. How can truth make reason understand the true knowledge of God? In his 17th chapter John said: "This is eternal life, to know thee the only true God." The world has as many gods as there are stars in the sky. They have brought truth down into many isms; but to have eternal life, you must know the only true God. The evangelist, John, then added the words: "and Jesus Christ whom thou hast sent."

There is only one pattern, only one path, which will lead you to sacred history —which is the same forever and ever. There is nothing accurate, however, about secular history. Two accounts of a little section of the last world war differ from each other. Eisenhower's son wrote a book about his father's experience, and Mr. Montgomery – General Eisenhower's right-hand man – wrote about the same experience, yet they are entirely different.

There is never any need to add to or take away from the Word of God. If, at the present time you do not understand it, just leave it as it is, for the day will come when you will. On that day the Living Word will unfold in you and interpret the written word, and you won't have to add to it or change it in any way. Scholars without vision have tried to change the word to make it conform to what they think, but do not know! As Paul said to the Galatians: "I notice you observe weeks, months, seasons, and years. I'm afraid I have labored over you in vain." There are not special weeks, months, seasons, or years; for you awakening can happen at any moment in time. The crucifixion began before that the world was, while Easter comes when the age of Caesar has reached its end. Resurrection is one side of the coin of Easter, with your birth from above as the other.

God sent his Word into your mind. That Word cannot return to him void, but must accomplish that which God purposed, and prosper in the thing for which it was sent. You will return claiming: "I have finished the work thou gavest me to do." God gave you only one thing to do, and that is to testify to the truth of his Word. You did not come here to make a lot of money, leave your name in granite, or your face carved on a mountainside. You did not come to change, judge, or condemn anything. Leave the world just as it is, for God planned

What is Truth?

everything as it has come out and as it will be consummated. Simply set your hope fully upon the grace that is coming to you, for you have come to bear witness to the truth. Nothing else! God's Word is truth, so you have come to fulfill scripture.

Now let us go into the silence.

Also Available From This Publisher

All Things Are Possible
ISBN 978-1-60386-740-5

Invisible Helpers
ISBN 978-1-60386-741-2

A Divine Event and Other Essays
ISBN 978-1-60386-742-9

An Assured Understanding & Other Sermons
ISBN 978-1-60386-743-6

Behold the Dreamer Cometh
ISBN 978-1-60386-744-3

Christ in You
ISBN 978-1-60386-722-1

The Way to the Kingdom
ISBN 978-1-60386-720-7

The Way Out
ISBN 978-1-60386-715-3

The Necessity of Prayer
ISBN 978-1-60386-714-6

Christ in You
ISBN 978-1-60386-710-8

The Golden Key & 22 Essays
ISBN 978-1-60386-706-1

At Your Command
ISBN 978-1-60386-677-4

You Can Never Outgrow I Am
ISBN 978-1-60386-676-7

Neville Goddard: The Essential Collection
978-1-60386-678-1

Ingram Content Group UK Ltd.
Milton Keynes UK
UKHW010815260623
424053UK00004B/425